THE ROYAL COURT THEATRE PRESENTS

Word-Play

by Rabiah Hussain

Word-Play was first performed at the Royal Court Jerwood Theatre
Upstairs, Sloane Square, on Thursday 20 July 2023.

Word-Play
by Rabiah Hussain

Cast (in alphabetical order)

Issam Al Ghussain
Kosar Ali
Simon Manyonda
Sirine Saba
Yusra Warsama

Director **Nimmo Ismail**
Designer **Rosanna Vize**
Lighting Designer **Jamie Platt**
Composer & Sound Designer **XANA**
Movement Director **Ken Nakajima**
Casting Director **Isabella Odoffin CDG**
Assistant Director **Aneesha Srinivasan**
Associate Designer **Alys Whitehead**
Consultant **Suhaiymah Manzoor-Khan**
Voice Coach **Emma Woodvine**
Production Manager **Phoebe Bath**
Stage Managers **Aiman Bandali, Suneeda Maruthiyil, Ava G. McCarthy
& Marie-Angelique St. Hill**
Artist Wellbeing Practitioner **Carol Cumberbatch**
Playwright's Personal Assistant **Pia Richards-Glöckner**
Set built by **Royal Court Stage Department & Ridiculous Solutions**

From the Royal Court, on this production:

Stage Supervisor **TJ Chappell-Meade**
Lighting Supervisor **Max Cherry**
Lead Producer **Chris James**
Costume Supervisor **Katie Price**
Lighting Programmer **Stephen Settle**
Sound Supervisor **Jet Sharp**
Company Manager **Mica Taylor**

The Royal Court Theatre and Stage Management wish to thank the following for their help with this production:
Chris Campbell, Oscar Sale.

Rabiah Hussain (Writer)

For the Royal Court: **One Night Stand with... Rabiah Hussain.**

Other theatre includes: **Spun (Arcola/Canada/Germany), Where I Live and What I Live For (Theatre Absolute).**

Awards include: **German Baden-Wuttemberg Youth Theatre Price (Spun), German Youth Theatre Award (Spun).**

Rabiah was selected as a writer for the Kudos TV and Royal Court Theatre Fellowship Programme 2019 and wrote on the third edition of the Royal Court Living Newspaper. She wrote WE ARE SHADOWS, an audio drama tour of Brick Lane for Tamasha Theatre. Rabiah was selected to be part of the BBC TV Drama Writers' Programme 2020.

Issam Al Ghussain (Cast)

Theatre includes: **King Lear, Macbeth (Globe); The Three Seagulls (Bristol Old Vic); Hide and Seek (Vaults Festival).**

Television includes: **Doctors, The Beaker Girls.**

Film includes: **Typist Artist Pirate King.**

Kosar Ali (Cast)

Television includes: **Dangerous Liaisons, Pru.**

Film includes: **Rocks, Muna, Luna.**

Awards include: **BIFA award for Best Supporting Actress (Rocks), BIFA Award for Most Promising Newcomer (Rocks), Muslim Women Award in Arts & Entertainment 2021, Screen International's Stars of Tomorrow 2021.**

Aiman Bandali
(Stage Manager - Book)

As production manager or production assistant, theatre includes: **Don Carlos, Love Steals Us from Loneliness (Carne); New England (Linbury Studio); Dick Whittington and his Cat [placement] (Lighthouse/Poole).**

As company manager or technical stage manager: **Rules for Living (Carne); Little Shop of Horrors, Earthquakes in London (Sainsbury Theatre).**

As stage manager on book or deputy stage manager: **My Brother's Keeper (Theatre503); Minding the Gap Project (Kiln); Three Day in the Country (Sainsbury Theatre).**

As assistant stage manager or assistant stage manager on book: **Hakawatis: The Women of the Arabian Nights (Sam Wanamaker); The Darkest Part of the Night (Kiln); Scandaltown (Lyric**

Hammersmith); **A Midsummers Night's Dream [placement] (Regent's Park Open Air); Uncle Vanya, I & You [placement] (Hampstead); Twelfth Night (Sainsbury Theatre).**

Phoebe Bath (Production Manager)

As production manager, theatre includes: **Noises Off (Theatre Royal Bath/Tour/West End); Saving Grace (Riverside); The Contingency Plan (Sheffield Crucible); Akedah, Further Education, R&D, Experience (Hampstead).**

As associate production manager, theatre includes: **Hey Duggee (Cuffe&Taylor/Kenny Wax/UK Tour); Patriots, Magic Goes Wrong, Groan Ups (& UK tour), Mischief Movie Night (& Riverside) (West End); Private Peaceful (Jonathan Church/UK Tour); Cluedo (JAS/UK Tour).**

Nimmo Ismail (Director)

As assistant director, for the Royal Court: **The Prudes, Goats.**

As director, theatre includes: **Two Billion Beats (Orange Tree); Glee & Me, Holding Space, The Christmas Star (Royal Exchange, Manchester); a meal (Poleroid); Fragments, My England (Young Vic); SNAP (Old Vic); two Palestinians go dogging (Sparkhaus); The Other Day, Twelve Months' Notice, The Debate, Winter Blossom Karaoke (Camden People's Theatre); Television Guide, The Displaced/We Came in a Tiny Red Boat, I Actually Have a Son (GSMD/Squint).**

As associate/assistant director, theatre includes: **Brokeback Mountain (West End); Phaedra, The Antipodes (National); Oklahoma!, Wings (Young Vic); Shedding a Skin (Soho); Our Town (Regent's Park Open Air); A Very Very Very Dark Matter (Bridge); The Phlebotomist (Hampstead); Quarter Life Crisis (Brixton House/Edinburgh Fringe).**

Nimmo took part in the Royal Court Writers Programme and is Sky Arts Artistic Associate at Theatre Royal Stratford East 2022/2023.

Simon Manyonda (Cast)

Theatre includes: **The Clinic (Almeida); Far Away, The Way of the World (Donmar); Actually (Trafalgar Studios); Alys, Always (Bridge); Barber Shop Chronicles, Light Shining in Buckinghamshire, King Lear, Greenland, Welcome to Thebes (National); King Lear (Old Vic); Giving, Wildefire (Hampstead); A Midsummer Nights Dreaming, Julius Caesar (RSC); A Midsummer Nights Dream (Lyric Hammersmith).**

Television includes: **Eric, Pennyworth, Van Der Valk, The Bay, His Dark Materials, King Lear, Shakespeare and Hathaway, Uncle, Neil Gaimans Likely Stories, Doctor Who, Suspects, Whitechapel.**

Film includes: **Northern Comfort, Rye Lane, The Witches, Undergods, In Fabric, The Current War, Jawbone, World War Z, Julius Caesar, How It's Done.**

Suhaiymah Manzoor-Khan
(Consultant)

As writer, for the Royal Court: **Living Newspaper #1.**

As writer, theatre includes: **A Coin In Somebody Else's Pocket (Uncut); The Tigers Come at Night (Freedom); For Brown Boys who Date White Girls (part of My White Best Friend (and other letters left unsaid)) (Bunker); End of Diaspora (Free Word Centre).**

As writer, poetry and prose includes: **Postcolonial Banter, Tangled In Terror: Uprooting Islamophobia, A FLY Girl's Guide To University: Being a woman of colour at Cambridge and other institutions of power and elitism [co-author], I Refuse to Condemn: resisting racism in times of national security [essayist], Cut From The Same Cloth? [essayist].**

Suneeda Maruthiyil
(Stage Manager - Props)

The following roles include prop making/sourcing and set building.

As production manager, theatre includes: **Dying For It (ALRA); Romeo and Juliet (Shakespeare In The Square); Leaper (Tucked In); The Magic Paintbrush, Into The Forest (Theatre Peckham); Islington The Opera (Young Actors Theatre).**

As company/technical stage manager, theatre includes: **Twist (Theatre Centre); Tamburlaine, Why The Lion Danced [CSM – cover] (New Earth); The Jury (Millfield); The Jungle Book (Sixteen Feet); Merchant of Venice (Studio 3 Arts); Sprung (Kazzum); The Local Stigmatic (Méliès); Land of Lights (Olly Cart); As You Like It, The Merry Wives of Windsor, A Midsummer Night's Dream, Colonel Blood And The Raven (Oxford Shakespeare Company); Hungry (Y-touring); Alice's Adventures In Wonderland (Open Book); Evita (Young Actors Theatre); The Great Gatsby, Hutch [in rep CSM – Riverside Studios], Bonnie & Clyde (Ruby In The Dust); Dead Funny (JBall); The Last Pearly (Pinhole); 1888 (Okai Collier Company); Judenfrei (Historia).**

As stage manager, theatre includes: **Widows (British American Drama Academy); Newspaper Boy and Origami Girl (Theatre Peckham); Daisy Pulls It Off, Twelfth Night, Skin Of Our Teeth (LOST); Our Boys (Tabard); Permission (Courtyard Studio); 99 Comedy Club [Casual SM].**

Lighting Design & Op: **Oxford Shakespeare Company, Dance Lab, Catch A Sea Star Lighting.**
Re-lighter & Op: **Twist, Leaper.**

For sound/AV, theatre includes: **Hungry (tech set up and operator); Islington The Opera (radio mics/live sound op)**
As technician, theatre includes: **Inside Out Festival (Somerset House Education Team).**

As assistant/deputy stage manager, theatre includes: **City Of The Unexpected (National Theatre Wales); Navrattan (UK Mela & Festival tour); BABEL (Wildworks/BAC); Billy The Kid (Unicorn); Desert Boy (Nitro); Mountview Acting Showcase (Criterion); The Pleasance Venues [Crew/Front of House] (Edinburgh Fringe); The Duchess of Malfi (Punchdrunk).**

Awards include: **SMA Best Team 2017 Cardiff (City of the Unexpected).**

Ava G. McCarthy
(Stage Manager Cover - Book)

For the Royal Court: **One Night Stands.**

As stage manager, theatre includes: **Cypress Dust Witch (Etcetera).**

As LX/Sound operator, theatre includes: **Shiny Things (2Northdown); Film Club (Museum of Comedy); Avocado (Barons Court); Lippy Drag Show, Fringe Preview (Glory); Fringe Preview (Castle).**

Ken Nakajima
(Movement Director & Choreographer)

Theatre includes: **Guidelines (Camden People's Theatre); Pore (Colour Factory).**

Film includes: **I Am Your Daughter (Florence Rose), SIRPLUS SS23, MACHINE-A SS23.**

Isabella Odoffin (Casting Director)

As casting director, theatre includes: **Beautiful Thing, After the End, Extinct, The Sun, the Moon and the Stars, Sucker Punch (Stratford East); The Collaboration, Klippies, In A Word (Young Vic); All of Us, Master Harold & the Boys, Three Sisters, Small Island [and remount] (National); Moreno (Theatre503); J'Ouvert (West End); Antigone: The Burial at Thebes (Lyric Hammersmith); A Taste of Honey (NTP);**

As casting director, TV and film includes:
Transamazonia, How to Have Sex, Supacell, Anansi Boys, I Used to be Famous, Girl, Boxing Day, ear for eye, The Last Bus, Blue Story.

As casting associate, TV and film includes: **Mary Queen of Scots, The Favourite, Baghdad in my Shadow, Beirut, Jawbone, Denial, This Beautiful Fantastic, Pan, Get Santa, Madame Bovary.**

As casting assistant, TV and film includes: **You, Me & The Apocalypse, Lady Chatterley's Lover, Sherlock Christmas Special.**

Jamie Platt (Lighting Designer)

As lighting designer, theatre includes: **The Last Five Years (West End); Jellyfish (National); Kes (Octagon & Theatre by the Lake); Suddenly Last Summer, Sister Act (English Theatre Frankfurt); Kinky Boots (New Wolsey); Something In the Air (Jermyn Street); RIDE (& Leicester Curve), The Last Five Years, Beast, Klippies (Southwark Playhouse); Mythic (Charing Cross); Either, Paradise, Yous Two (Hampstead); Anna Karenina (Silk St.); SUS, Never Not Once, Gently Down The Stream, Alkaline (Park); Moonlight and Magnolias (Nottingham Playhouse); Le Grand Mort (Trafalgar Studios); Beauty and the Beast, Absurd Person Singular (Watford Palace); The Beat of our Hearts (Northcott); Singin' In the Rain (The Mill at Sonning); Sonny, Once On This Island (ArtsEd); Blood Orange, The Moor, Where Do Little Birds Go? (Old Red Lion); One Who Wants to Cross, Checkpoint Chana, Quaint Honour, P'yongyang, We Know Where You Live, Chicken Dust (Finborough); Head Over Heels, Vincent River (Hope Mill); Pattern Recognition (Platform & world tour); Reared, Screwed, Grey Man (Theatre503); The Trap (Omnibus).**

As lighting designer, opera includes: **The Barber of Seville (Nevill Holt Opera).**

As associate lighting designer, theatre includes: **Frozen, (& International) SIX (& International), INK, The Night of the Iguana, The Starry Messenger, Bitter Wheat (West End); Albion, The Hunt, Three Sisters, Machinal (Almeida); Piaf (Teatro Liceo, Buenos Aires).**

Sirine Saba (Cast)

For the Royal Court: **The Crossing Plays, Goats, Fireworks.**

Other theatre includes: **Phaedra, Another World, Nation, Sparkleshark (National); Britannicus (Lyric Hammersmith); Romeo and Juliet, The Winter's Tale, King Lear, Antony and Cleopatra, Holy Warriors (Globe); Why It's Kicking Off Everywhere (Young Vic); The Haystack, Botticelli in the Fire, The Intelligent Homosexual's Guide to Capitalism and Socialism With a Key to the Scriptures (Hampstead); Wife, Testing the Echo (& Out of Joint) (Kiln); The Invisible (Bush); Next Fall (Southwark Playhouse); The Winter's Tale, The Taming of the Shrew, A Midsummer Night's Dream, Twelfth Night, HMS Pinafore (Regent's Park Open Air), Scorched (Old Vic); Baghdad Wedding (Soho); Beauty and the Beast, Midnight's Children, The Tempest, The Winter's Tale, Pericles, A Midsummer Night's Dream, Tales from Ovid (& Young Vic), A Warwickshire Testimony (RSC); Rogers and Hammerstein's Cinderella (Bristol Old Vic).**
TV includes: **Beyond Paradise, Midsomer Murders, Doctor Who, Holby City, Cleaning Up, Why It's Kicking off Everywhere, EastEnders, Unforgotten, Doctors, Silent Witness, I am Slave, Footballers' Wives, The Bill, Prometheus.**

Film includes: **The Black Forest, Maestro, Exhibition, Death of the Revolution.**

Radio/audio includes: **Mother Courage, The Passport, The Medici, Slime, Savages, Tumanbay, Wide Sargasso Sea, The Brick, The Insider, Colour Inside the Lines, Descent.**

Aneesha Srinivasan
(Assistant Director)

As director, theatre includes: **Brown Girls Do It Too [co-director] (& UK tour), Before I Was A Bear (& Bunker) (Soho); The Woman in the Film (Roundhouse).**

As assistant director, theatre includes: **Name, Place, Animal, Thing (Almeida).**

Marie-Angelique St. Hill
(Stage Manager - Props)

For the Royal Court: **Graceland, For Black Boys Who Have Considered Suicide When The Hue Gets Too Heavy.**

As stage manager, other theatre includes: **Tambo & Bones (Stratford East); For Black Boys Who Have Considered Suicide When The Hue Gets Too Heavy (West End); REP Season (Training) (National Youth); 5 Plays (Young Vic).**

As assistant stage manager, for the Royal Court: **A Kind of People.**

As assistant stage manager, other theatre includes: **Dirty Dancing (Secret Cinema); Hamlet, Tree (Young Vic/& MIF); Aladdin (Hackney Empire); In the night garden tour (Minor Entertainment).**

Rosanna Vize (Designer)

Theatre credits include: **Julius Caesar, Earthworks and Myth (RSC); Glass Menagerie (Royal Exchange); Britannicus (Lyric Hammersmith); Brown Girls Do It Too, Shedding A Skin, Girls (& Hightide/Talawa) (Soho); Mavra and Pierrot Lunaire (ROH); Gulliver's Travels (Unicorn); Camp Siegfried, Midsummer Party (Old Vic); Cat On A Hot Tin Roof (Leicester Curve/UK tour); The Two Character Play, The Phlebotomist, Yous Two (Hampstead); The Enemy (National Scotland); Harm, An Adventure, Leave Taking (Bush); The Comeback (West End); Incantata (Irish Rep, NYC/Galway); Hedda Gabler (Sherman); The Audience (Nuffield Theatre); Don Carlos (Exeter Northcott); The Almighty Sometimes (Royal Exchange); King Lear (Globe); Low Level Panic (Orange Tree); After October (Finborough); Henry I (Reading Between the Lines).**

TV/film includes: **Harm, Wake Me Up.**

Yusra Warsama (Cast)

Theatre credits include: **Nora: A Doll's House, The Sound of Silence (Royal Exchange); The Vote (Donmar); Future Bodies, On Corporation Street (HOME); The Claim (Shoreditch Town Hall); An Injury (Ovalhouse); Shared Memories (& Kali), The Crows Plucked Your Sinews (& Bush/UK tour) (Curve); Crystal Kisses (Contact); Bolt-Holed (Birmingham Rep); Aisha (National).**

As writer, credits include: **Of All the Beautiful Things in the World (HOME); My White Best Friend North (Royal Exchange).**

TV and film includes: **The Gallows Pole, Unforgotten, Castle Rock, Cold Feet, Call the Midwife, Our Girl, The Journey is the Destination, Last Days on Mars.**

Radio and voice work includes: **Mirror Mirror, Gaia, 24 Hours of Peace, Odour, This is Your Country Too, Quake.**

Alys Whitehead
(Associate Designer)

As designer, theatre includes: **Snowflakes (Park); The Retreat (Finborough); Lysistrata (Lyric Hammersmith); SAD (Omnibus); Maddie (Arcola).**

As associate designer, theatre includes: **Zoe's Peculiar Journey Through Time (Theatre Rites/Southbank Centre & International Tour); Sea Creatures (Hampstead).**

As assistant designer, theatre includes: **Dixon and Daughters (National).**

Emma Woodvine (Voice Coach)

For the Royal Court: **Inside Bitch, Pigs and Dogs, Hang, Routes.**

Other theatre includes: **Julius Caesar, As You Like It, Midsummer Night's Dream, The Tempest, Swive (Globe); A Little Night Music, Street Scene, Kiss Me Kate, Carousel, The Magic Flute (Opera North); Fun Home, Scotsboro' Boys, Wings, Happy Days, Galileo, A Streetcar Named Desire, A Season in the Congo, A Doll's House, The Mountain, The Changeling, Beloved (Young Vic); The Trials (Donmar); Machinal (Almeida); Cymbeline, Imperium Part I and II, Richard II, Henry IV Parts I and II, Henry V, Two Gentlemen of Verona, The Witch of Edmonton, Loves Sacrifice, The Jew of Malta (RSC); Yeoman of the Guard (ENO); Gypsy, Twelfth Night (Royal Exchange); Tom Fool, 2 Billion Heartbeats, When the Sun Shines, Blood Knot (Orange Tree); Fishermans Friends the Musical (International Tour); The Audience, Glass Menagerie (Nuffield Theatre); The Winter's Tale, 'Tis Pity She's a Whore, Macbeth (Cheek by Jowl); Beautiful: the Carole King Musical (UK Tour); Ghost the Musical (West End); Aladdin, Dick Whittington (Lyric Hammersmith); Hello and Goodbye (York Theatre Royal); Pitchfork Disney (Arcola); The School for Scandal (Barbican); 11 and 12 (Peter Brook).**

Film includes: **CLICQUOT, Demon 79, BLACK MIRROR, CYRANO, Darkest Hour, Jesus His Life, Christopher and His Kind.**

XANA (Composer & Sound Designer)

For the Royal Court: **Living Newspaper #4.**

Other theatre includes: **Anna Karenina (Edinburgh Lyceum/Bristol Old Vic); Galatea (Emma Frankland, Wildworks, Marlborough Productions); Hamnet (RSC); The Trials, Mary Seacole (Donmar); Sundown Kiki, Changing Destiny, Fairview, Ivan and the Dogs, The Collaboration (Young Vic); ...cake (Theatre Peckham); Who Killed My Father (Tron/Scotland tour); as british as a watermelon (Contact); Hyde and Seek (Guildhall); Sleepova, The P Word, Strange Fruit (Bush); Burgerz (Hackney Showroom); Black Holes (The Place); Sankofa: Before the Whitewash, Hive City Legacy (Roundhouse); Glamrou: From Quran to Queen, Curious, Half-Breed (Soho); Blood Knot (Orange Tree); Noughts and Crosses (Pilot).**

THE ROYAL COURT THEATRE

The Royal Court Theatre is the writers' theatre. It is a leading force in world theatre for cultivating and supporting writers – undiscovered, emerging and established.

Through the writers, the Royal Court is at the forefront of creating restless, alert, provocative theatre about now. We open our doors to the unheard voices and free thinkers that, through their writing, change our way of seeing.

Over 120,000 people visit the Royal Court in Sloane Square, London, each year and many thousands more see our work elsewhere through transfers to the West End and New York, UK and international tours, digital platforms, our residencies across London, and our site-specific work. Through all our work we strive to inspire audiences and influence future writers with radical thinking and provocative discussion.

The Royal Court's extensive development activity encompasses a diverse range of writers and artists and includes an ongoing programme of writers' attachments, readings, workshops and playwriting groups. Twenty years of the International Department's pioneering work around the world means the Royal Court has relationships with writers on every continent.

Since 1956 we have commissioned and produced hundreds of writers, from John Osborne to Jasmine Lee-Jones. Royal Court plays from every decade are now performed on stage and taught in classrooms and universities across the globe.

We strive to create an environment in which differing voices and opinions can co-exist. In current times, it is becoming increasingly difficult for writers to write what they want or need to write without fear, and we will do everything we can to rise above a narrowing of viewpoints.

It is because of this commitment to the writer and our future that we believe there is no more important theatre in the world than the Royal Court.

 royalcourt ☐ royalcourttheatre

Supported using public funding by
ARTS COUNCIL ENGLAND

ROYAL

ASSISTED PERFORMANCES

Captioned Performances

Captioned performances are accessible for people who are D/deaf, deafened & hard of hearing, as well as being suitable for people for whom English is not a first language.

Cuckoo
Wednesday 2nd August 2023, 7:30pm
Thursday 3rd August 2023, 2:30pm
Saturday 12th August 2023, 2:30pm

Word-Play
Wednesday 16th August 2023, 7:45pm
Saturday 26th August 2023, 3pm

Imposter 22
Thursday 12th October, 7:30pm

Blue Mist
Thursday 9th November, 7:45pm
Friday 10th November, 7:45pm

Mates in Chelsea
Wednesday 6th December, 7:30pm
Thursday 7th December, 2:30pm

BSL-interpreted Performances

BSL-interpreted performances, delivered by an interpreter, give a sign inteprretation of the text spoken and/or sung by artists in the onstage production.

Cuckoo
Saturday 19th August 2023, 2:30pm

Imposter 22
Friday 13th October, 7:30pm

Mates in Chelsea
Saturday 2nd December, 2:30pm

COURT

ROYAL

ASSISTED PERFORMANCES

Performances in a Relaxed Environment

Relaxed Environment performances are suitable for those who may benefit from a more relaxed environment.

During these performances:
- There is a relaxed attitude to noise in the auditorium; you are welcome to respond to the show in whatever way feels natural
- You can enter and exit the auditorium when needed
- We will help you find the best seats for your experience
- House lights may remain raised slightly
- Loud noises may be reduced

Cuckoo
Saturday 12th August, 2:30pm

Word-Play
Saturday 19th August, 3pm

Imposter 22
All performances are relaxed.

Blue Mist
Saturday 11th November, 7:45pm

Mates in Chelsea
Saturday 9th December, 2:30pm

If you would like to talk to us about your access requirements, please contact our Box Office at (0)20 7565 5000 or boxoffice@royalcourttheatre.com

The Royal Court Visual Story is available on our website. Story and Sensory synposes are available on the show pages via the Whats On tab of the website shortly after Press Night.

COURT

ROYAL COURT SUPPORTERS

Our incredible community of supporters makes it possible for us to achieve our mission of nurturing and platforming writers at every stage of their careers. Our supporters are part of our essential fabric – they help to give us the freedom to take bigger and bolder risks in our work, develop and empower new voices, and create world-class theatre that challenges and disrupts the theatre ecology.

To all our supporters, thank you. You help us to write the future.

PUBLIC FUNDING

Supported using public funding by
ARTS COUNCIL ENGLAND

CHARITABLE PARTNERS

BackstageTrust

JERWOOD ARTS

CORPORATE SPONSORS

Aqua Financial Ltd
Cadogan
Edwardian Hotels, London
Sustainable Wine Solutions
The Sloane Club
Walpole

SIS TER

CORPORATE MEMBERS

Bloomberg Philanthopies
Sloane Stanley

TRUSTS AND FOUNDATIONS

Martin Bowley Charitable Trust
The Noël Coward Foundation
Cowley Charitable Foundation
The D'Oyly Carte Charitable Trust
The Lynne Gagliano Writer's Award
The Golden Bottle Trust
John Lyon's Charity
Clare McIntyre's Bursary
Old Possum's Practical Trust
The Austin and Hope Pilkington Trust
Richard Radcliffe Charitable Trust
Rose Foundation
John Thaw Foundation
The Victoria Wood Foundation

ROYAL

BAR & KITCHEN

The Royal Court's Bar & Kitchen aims to create a welcoming and inspiring environment with a style and ethos that reflects the work we put on stage.

Offering expertly crafted cocktails alongside an extensive selection of craft gins and beers, wine and soft drinks, our vibrant basement bar provides a sanctuary in the middle of Sloane Square. By day a perfect spot for meetings or quiet reflection and by night atmospheric meeting spaces for cast, crew, audiences and the general public.

All profits go directly to supporting the work of the Royal Court theatre, cultivating and supporting writers – undiscovered, emerging and established.

For more information, visit
royalcourttheatre.com/bar

HIRES & EVENTS

The Royal Court is available to hire for celebrations, rehearsals, meetings, filming, ceremonies and much more. Our two theatre spaces can be hired for conferences and showcases, and the building is a unique venue for bespoke events and receptions.

For more information, visit
royalcourttheatre.com/events

Sloane Square London, SW1W 8AS ⊖ Sloane Square ⇌ Victoria Station
🐦 royalcourt 🆕 theroyalcourttheatre 📷 royalcourttheatre

COURT

SUPPORT THE COURT AND BE A PART OF OUR FUTURE.

Our Friends and Good Friends are part of the fabric of the Royal Court. They are our regulars and together, we enjoy bold and restless theatre that provokes and challenges us all. Like all friends, they help us too. The income we receive from our memberships directly supports our mission, providing writers with the space and platform to experiment and develop their writing.

Become a Friend today and inspire the next generation of theatre makers.

Become a Friend (from £40 a year)

Benefits include:
- Priority Booking
- Advanced access to £12 Monday tickets for productions in the Jerwood Theatre Downstairs
- 10% discount in our Bar & Kitchen (including Court in the Square) and Samuel French bookshop

Become a Good Friend (from £95 a year)

Our Good Friends' membership also includes a voluntary donation. This extra support goes directly towards supporting our work and future, both on and off stage.

In addition to the Friend benefits, our Good Friends also receive:
- Five complimentary playtexts for Royal Court productions
- An invitation for two to step behind the scenes of the Rpyal Court Theatre at a special annual event

To become a Friend or a Good Friend, or to find out more about the different ways in which you can get involved, visit our website: royalcourttheatre.com/support-us

The English Stage Company at the Royal Court Theatre is a registered charity (No. 231242)

WORD-PLAY

Rabiah Hussain

Introduction
Rabiah Hussain

In writing this play about language, my life took a pretty funny turn... I discovered that I had a brain tumour, and as a result of a major operation to remove it, I developed aphasia – a language disorder which affects your ability to read, write, speak, and also understand words.

I remember even losing the *feeling* of words... I don't know if that even makes sense. But it may have something to do with how strongly I associate language with emotion. Something I know we can all relate to.

Thankfully, over time, my words came back to me. I still live with mild aphasia, but I don't mind. Because where I sometimes have difficulty remembering words, at least I'm not living with the emptiness of having access to only a handful of them. This stays with me as a reminder of how powerful language really can be.

For all intents and purposes, *Word-Play* is, at its heart, about this same power of language. Where language has the power to connect you to emotions, it also has the power to change the course of society. And *Word-Play* examines this in relation to the political landscape and structures that adopt it.

So much about language can be instinctive. I know for me, when writing, first comes the basic idea, then the feeling I want to convey, and the language patterns respond to that. And that is why *Word-Play* doesn't adopt linear storytelling with extensive character backstories. Instead, we sit in the spaces in-between. Where language can be unpacked and the feeling of words can weave their way through the various scenes.

In the weaving of words, linguistic patterns emerge. Sometimes semantics are at the forefront, so words are stripped of context. At other times, they are rooted within it, so we see the real-life impact that political language can have on wider society.

There are moments where the meaning of words is questioned directly. How do you explain a throwaway comment? What is throwaway really? And how are words interpreted by people based on their experience?

It's this experience of words and language that the play continues to explore. From first language acquisition to multilingual stress and the code-switching that can accompany it. Alongside this sits the raw emotions related to having a mother tongue, where the language of your childhood may not be your first any more, but it still lives and floats around in your body.

Of course, despite the recognised benefits of multilingualism, languages are put in a hierarchy, and then used in political conversations around citizenship. When policy around language is changed and shifted to equate language with how 'good' a citizen you are, we arrive in a place where verbal stones are thrown at certain communities, who are then asked to forgo their mother tongues for the more 'progressive' and 'normal' languages of the countries they now live in. Multilingualism becomes a negative thing. And it is monolingualism that is then tied to nationalism.

These things don't simply sit outside of ourselves. Politics has real-life effect. It has an emotional and physical impact. Words accumulate and gather collective weight. They remove and stir us. And where we turn to language to help us convey what we are thinking, language can also be manipulated. It is the architecture of political language and its impact that *Word-Play* is unpacking.

Language in all its forms – written, sign, spoken, heard, seen – is something that lives and breathes. Language is not a linear, static thing. It moves and changes. It can be pulled and shaped depending on the effect it is to lead. It's beautiful and ugly. It's ever shifting and is usually the first place where change happens. This is what makes it essential. And this is why those in power focus on it so much.

4

Acknowledgements

As well as the team who have brought *Word-Play* to the stage, I'd also like to thank the following people who have helped at various stages of the production.

Noelle Adames, Nick Barron, Milli Bhatia, Jane Fallowfield, Vicky Featherstone, Ellie Fulcher, Alex Constantin, Jasmyn Fisher-Ryner, Dr Agnieszka Lyons, Suhaiymah Manzoor-Khan, Lucy Morrison, Fran O'Donnell, Lettie Precious, Tomás Palmer, Pia Richards, Nicole Schivardi, Rosie Thackeray, debbie tucker green, Daberechi Ukoha-Kalu, Ragevan Vasan, Ross Willis, Melanie Wilson.

Thank you also to all the actors during the various points in development.

R.H.

To Saadi.
For helping me find my words again.

Notes on Text

The characters in each scene are different with the exception of No. 10 Press Office 11 a.m., No. 10 Press Office 11 p.m., Normal 1, Normal 2 and Normal 3, which are recurring scenes.

' – ' indicates a quick response between lines.

Italics indicates emphasised words.

Beat indicates a short pause.

'…' indicates a continuing thought and/or a short pause.

' / ' indicates an interjection or interruption of a line.

'<u>Underlining</u>' indicates a heavily emphasised word.

Alphabets used in **BONES** – Urdu, Arabic, Somali, Farsi.

This text went to press before the end of rehearsals and so may differ slightly from the play as performed.

RIVERS OF BLOOD

Characters: A (*male*), B (*male*).

A   This is a moment.

B   It *is* a moment.

A   A moment to remember –

B   – A moment *to* remember.

A   Will it be?

B   What?

A   Remembered.

B   It should be –

A   – Should?

B   It *could* be.

    Beat.

A   *Could* indicates that you don't believe it *will* be.

B   I believe it *should* be talked about. And it *could* be talked about. But –

A   – But what?

B   I'm *simply* going by history.

A   It's a considerable moment. *In* history.

B   *Sometimes* even *considerable* moments end up relegated to textbooks.

A   Surely it's *bigger* than that?

B   So *much* bigger.

A   It created something. *Unity* –

B   – Chaos.

A   *Good* chaos –

B   – Life-*altering* chaos. I *agree*.

A   Then surely it *is*, *should* be and *will* be talked about.

B   I'm simply saying that sometimes, *sometimes*, these
         events that *feel*, and *are* a *moment* for those of us who
         are experiencing them in the *here* and *now*, can *also*
         remain a *moment* in the *memory* of *history* confined to
         our present. And *so*, can be seen by those in the *future*,
         as a moment *back* in time.

A   But this *isn't* and *shouldn't* be *just* a *moment* in the
         distant past for them.

B   I agree.

A   It should be *bigger*.

B   It *should* be bigger.

A   It should be *vast* –

B   – It should be a wave.

A   A wave?

B   A *wave*...

         Continuous. Sweeping. A moment that is so *alive* it
         echoes through time. *Oscillates*. Immerses with other
         waves in the *future* to create *multiple* moments so it can
         become *more* than *just* a *moment* in the distant past for
         them. We want it to be *felt*. Not *just* remembered...

A   ...And how do we ensure that happens?

B   We give it a name.

A   A *name*? It *has* a name.

B   No, no, no. Not a *name* that simply refers to *where* it
         happened. So many moments *have* happened and *will*
         happen in that place. There will be *hundreds* of moments
         there.

A   Then *his* name. The one who *created* the moment.

B   It's not enough. Imagine *years* down the line. People forget the names of presidents. Of celebrities. Of *prophets*! But *we*, as people, *are* what we do. And what we *do can* be remembered, *even* if our name isn't.

     Beat.

A   So, what kind of name do we give it?

B   A *name* that will *survive* the *test* of *time. A name* with a *physicality*. Something that conjures up an image. An *imprint. A presence* in people's minds. A name that says it is *bigger* than itself. That says it is *alive*! Not just in pictures and history books. But in their *bodies*. In their *guts*!... A name that leaves a *legacy* in the public consciousness, *so* that it's *felt* by *every* generation in the *future* as *their present*.

A   'We Shall *Fight* on the Beaches...'

B   '*This* Was Their *Finest* Hour...'

A   'Segregation *Now*, Segregation *Tomorrow*...'

B   'The *Empire* On Which the Sun *Never* Sets!'

     Beat.

     A name that *stirs* the guts. Pits neighbour against neighbour. A name to turn tides back a *different* way for *generations*... Because history *always* ripples on. *Even* if we don't realise it. And the *ripples* after he threw that stone in the river *need* to be remembered... *Ripples* that become *waves*.

A   Ripples...

B   *Waves*...

A   Rivers...

B   Blood.

A   The rivers...

B   The *blood*...

A   Rivers…

B   *Rivers.*

A   Rivers of…

B   *Of…?*

A   Blood…

       Beat.

A/B   *Rivers of Blood.*

NO. 10 PRESS OFFICE

11 A.M.

Characters: A, B, C, D, E.

A, B, C *on stage.*

A   *Fucking* disaster!

B   It doesn't *have* to be.

A   It already *is*!

B   Don't be so dramatic.

A   *Dramatic?!* You're not *stupid.* You know what a *shitstorm* this will create.

B   We *simply* need to issue an apology from / him –

A   – *If* / we can find him.

B   Let's get it written first and *when* / he –

A   – *If* / he approves it!

B   *Then* we'll worry about finding him!

        D *enters.*

A   Any luck?

D   Still trying to get through to him.

A   Where the *fuck* did he go?

D   Got into the car and drove off apparently.

B   Have we called the driver?

D   It's not going through. But I'll keep trying.

        D *exits.*

A   He wants to make our lives hell.

B   I *doubt* he was thinking that. *When* he was saying it. I doubt he was thinking, '*Yes! This will make the team's lives hell!*'

A   Well, he *should've* been!

C   Shall I make notes?

Beat.

A   What?

C   Shall I start making notes?

A   No... not yet.

B   When everyone gets here.

C   Right, right. That's fine.

B   We don't want *us* slagging the PM off going into the notes, *do* we?

C   Of course. Sorry. I wasn't sure.

E *enters.*

E   Anything?

B   Still trying to get through to him.

E   Who was with him?

A   You know *who*.

B   *The-Secretary-of-State-for-all-things-shitty-in-this-country.*

C   Shall I *start* making notes?

A   No, not yet.

E   Tell me *exactly* what happened?

A   Once again he decided the briefing document wasn't *sufficient* enough. Started *ad-libbing*.

B   Have you heard the clip?

A   Yeah.

B   I know *you* have.

E   Put it on.

A   Can someone...

B *puts it on. They gather around a laptop.*

C   Shall I make notes *now*?

A   Fucking hell! Yes, okay. Fine. Start making notes.

B   It's on…

     They listen closely.

A   Look at his face! He knew as *soon* as he started saying it. But he couldn't *stop* himself.

E   *Who* has picked it up?

B   Some journos were there… A couple of people on Twitter.

A   It's *only* been ten minutes.

B   We've got another *ten minutes* before shit *really* hits the fan.

A   *What's* the course of action?

E   Keep trying to locate him. *Cancel* his next visit and *get him back here*. Answer to press calls is… '*PM statement on way.*' We issue a press release with an *apology*. And then… we let the storm pass.

     D *enters.*

D   He's not going to apologise.

A   What?!

D   He's heading back here. But '*no apology*' he said.

A   *Fuck!*

B   Okay, now he *is* trying to make our lives hell.

E   Time to call in some favours.

     E *leaves.*

A   We can't put *that* in the statement. 'The Prime Minister *shouldn't* have said it but *guess* what, no *bloody* apology from him!'

B   Okay, what about a *roundabout* apology? 'I'm sorry *if* my comments offended…'

D   No. We just about convinced him to release a statement. And he said we're *all* fired if the word '*sorry*' is written in it.

B   Now what?

A   Right, *you*...

C   *Me?*

A   Look up synonyms for 'sorry'.

B   *Synonyms* for 'sorry'? For god's sake!

A   He doesn't want us to say 'sorry' so we'll find an alternative.

C   Shall I stop making notes?

A   Just *do* what I've asked you to do!

A *and* C *around a laptop.*

C   Depressed, downcast, disheartened, dejected, despondent, *despairing*...

A   Despairing? These don't sound right...

C   Sorrowful, remorseful, repentant, wretched...

B   *Wretched?*

C   *Heart-rending*...

A   Idiot! You're looking at the *wrong* adjectives. These are for when you *feel* sorry for someone!

B   Okay, we could go for a simple '*my apologies*'. It's *not* '*sorry*'.

D   It's *too* close to 'sorry'.

A   What about *those* ones?

C   'Pardon', 'pardon me', 'I *beg* your pardon.'

A   He didn't belch.

C   An '*oops*'... or a '*whoops*'...?

A   Neither did he let one rip!

D   *Where* are you looking?

C   'Quirky Ways to Say Sorry.' We have slang options too.
        'Soz','Sowee', '*Mi-scusi*'…

B   …He's not Del Boy.

A   Keep looking!

C   Um… 'I eat humble pie'… 'We need to see other
        people'… 'George W. *Bush*'…

A   What's 'George W. Bush?' What that does even mean?!

C   'Sorry, world, *my bad.*'

D   Can we go back to *actual* synonyms.

C   Remorseful, repentant, rueful, mortified, conscience-
        stricken, *guilty*…

        Beat.

        Opposite is unrepentant or unsympathetic.

D   We're *not* using a synonym.

B   Okay, then we say the Prime Minster's words were taken
        out of context.

A   They were said on *live* TV!

B   Doesn't matter. No one watches *live* TV any more. We
        can start a rumour that it's edited wrong. Blame *AI* or
        something.

A   *No one* is buying that.

B   Okay, fine! The Prime Minister '*regrets*' if his words
        caused offence.

A   '*If*'?

B   Okay, '*that*'.

D   He won't let us use '*that*'.

B   Alright, stop for a minute. Listen to it again. What did he
        emphasise?

A   What do you mean?

B   What *word* did he *emphasise*?

A   I don't know.

B   Then *fucking* listen to it!

      They listen. E *returns at some point. Doesn't intervene straight away.*

D   He emphasised 'can'.

B   No, he emphasised 'seen'.

A   Which is worse to have emphasised?

B   I mean, '*can*' is better. It could be used to indicate someone *else's* opinion.

D   Yes, it's like saying, '*I* don't think that but someone else might.'

A   What about 'seen'?

D   It's more *knowing*. Betrays the fact that it's *your* opinion and *not* someone else's. So the '*can*' in the sentence becomes redundant.

E   He emphasised 'are'.

A   What?

E   He emphasised '*are*'.

A   Then we're screwed.

B   Yeah. We can't cover that up.

D   Okay, we have a problem…

B   What's happened?

D   Message from his team… 'Changed his mind. He's heading to the next visit. Soz…'

A   Pissing shit! What is *wrong* with the man!

B   He's insane!

A   What do we do?

E   We work on aesthetics.

A   Right. Right. A good photo op. Find a *holy* festival. Or send him to one of their places of worship.

B   Let's not go *that* far.

A   Get him a change of suit. *And* a hairbrush.

B   No, he looks more human with messy hair.

E   Where is he going now?

D   A school visit.

A   *Please* tell me it's in Bradford or something...

D   Shropshire.

A   For god's sake!

E   (*To* D.) Call around the departments. And remember. *Aesthetics*. So get the right-*looking* person.

D   Got it.

B   Done.

E   I'll get lines to him.

     B, D *and* E *leave*.

C   Do you want to read the notes?

A   No, I bloody don't. What else can we do?

C   Does he read Rumi?

A   Rumi? I don't know. Why?

C   We can tweet some Rumi quotes from him. They're always popular.

A   Which ones?

     C *searches*.

C   'Wherever you are, and whatever you do, be in love...'

A   He's on his third marriage. He'll take that *too* literally.

C   'Live life as if everything is rigged in your favour.'

A   *Really?* You want to give people a reason to pull at *that* thread? What's that one...

C   'Don't you know yet? It is your light that lights the
        world.'

A   *That's* an invite for comments on energy bills!
        Obviously, Rumi cannot help in this situation.

        B, D *and* E *return.*

D   A couple of them are available. But, of course…

B   …They're not of that faith.

E   Aesthetics. They'll have to do. What is it looking like
        online?

D   It's up on Guardian, BBC, Sky…

B   …*And* being commented on by bloggers who think
        they're journalists.

D   It's being called out by the community now too. The
        reps are demanding an apology.

E   Dig up all reports being done on diversity. And keep an
        eye on the polls.

B   More opposition tweets coming through…

A   Divert attention?

D   Anti-Semitism in *their* party?

E   Use that to bump down his search traffic.

B   Any other news we can distract the online crowd with?

D   Immigration…? Strikes…? Trade unions…?

E   Get our think tanks on it.

C   There's a recoupling on *Love Island* tonight…

A   You stick to making notes!

D   *Wait*… He's just got a tweet of support…

E   From?

D   *China*…

POLITICAL BOO-BOO

Characters: A, B.

A   What a *goof* –

B   – *Slip-up to make* –

A   – *Blooper*-reel stuff –

B   – *Complete* fail –

A   – He botched it –

B   – *Blundered* it –

A   – Nitwit –

B   – Bobble brain –

A   – Of *all* the *gaffes*!

B   *An utter* political boo-boo!

A   An ouch for *them*…

B   …A sweep for *us*.

CORPORATE CLICK-CLICK

Characters: A, B (*female*).

A   (*To* B.) *We* are *here* for you.
      You are important.

      No, no. Don't say a word.
      Not a *single* word.

      We *get* it.

      This is why *we* do what *we* do.
      And *you* do what *you* do.

      No, not a word.
      Not a *word*...
      You don't have to *say* a *single word*.

      Beat.

      If they can *see* you,
      They don't have to *hear* you.

      So, instead,
      Let's show the world.

      Represent.

      Sshhh. Sshhh. *Ssshhh*.
      Spit out the sadness.
      Go on, go on.
      Spit it out, spit it out...
      Spit it out.

      There we are.
      Isn't that better?

      You're beautiful.
      You're strong.
      And *now*...
      You're *empty*.

      So, let's stand straight.
      Look proud.
      Look loud.
      And *smile* for the camera.

      Beat.

      Click-click...

SO-WHAT RADIO

Characters: A, B, C.

Words in square brackets are said and heard, but attempted to cover over with a beep. C *can be seen and heard or simply heard.*

A   So, in *your* opinion, should we differentiate between what someone *says* and what they actually *mean*? Now, remember, we are talking solely about that. Just that. *Nothing* more.

B   Well, we can debate semantics all day. But certain words will undoubtedly have an impact. *Particularly*, if they are coming from *those* in *power*. And the comments of the Prime Minister today were a deliberate attempt to [inflame]...

    Beat.

    What was that?

A   Hm?

B   What was that sound?

A   What sound?

B   *That* sound. The *beep*.

A   Oh, you heard it...

    Beat.

    That was our Impartiality Beeper.

B   Your what?

A   Well, you almost gave an opinion. So, it went off.

B   I can't give an opinion?

A   We are an impartial media outlet.

B   But you played the Prime Minister's comments...

A   Yes.

B   ...And those defending him.

A   It was in the public interest.

B   Don't you think that's a little [weird]…?

      What was *that* for?!

A   Impartiality is *very* important to us.

B   But all I said is that it's [weird]. It's [*weird*] that you
      think the word [*weird*] isn't impartial! Can you stop
      bleeping out the word [*weird*]!

A   You're making it *very* difficult to be impartial.

B   But this is fucking [weird]!… So, I can say the word
      '*fucking*' but I can't say the word [*weird*]?!

A   I'd rather you didn't swear on my show.

B   That is fucking [*weirddddddd*]!

      A *cuts* B *off.*

A   Okay, thank you so much to our lovely guest who joined
      us today, but had to leave abruptly. We are now taking
      some calls. And the same question to our callers. The
      exact same question. Should we differentiate between
      what someone *says* and what they *mean*?… Yes, hello.
      What are your views on this, caller?

C   '*Yes. I'm calling to say that it requires a balance
      between both. Sometimes we say certain things, but
      mean something else. Other times, we say exactly what
      we mean. And so, it depends on the situation.*'

A   Thank you, caller. That is *exactly* the kind of impartiality
      we were looking for.

C   '*But I have a question…*'

A   Yes, caller. Go ahead.

C   '*So what?*'

      Beat.

A   Sorry?

C   '*My question is, so what? So what if he said it? So what
      if he meant it? So… what? So what?*'

NORMAL 1 – MORNING

Characters: A, B, C, D, E.

WhatsApp scene. This scene can be played simply as words being said in a group.

A   Share video link. (*Send.*) To cheer you all up this morning. (*Send.*)

B   Grimacing-face emoji. Hate cats. (*Send.*)

A   Search GIF: 'You're weird.' (*Send.*)

B   Search GIF: 'I am what I am.'(*Send.*)

A   Cats everywhere in Turkey. (*Send.*)

B   My worst nightmare. (*Send.*)

A   Treated like… crown emoji. I was in… heaven emoji. (*Send.*)

B   Scared-face emoji. (*Send.*)

C   Typing… Typing… Typing…

D   (*Voice-note recording.*) '…Cats are interesting. They know how to live peacefully in chaos.' (*Send.*)

E   (*Voice-note recording.*) 'Your way of telling us to be more cat-like today?' (*Send.*)

B   Can't stop… eating emoji… Today. Don't know why. (*Send.*)

E   Don't feel peaceful today though. I feel angry. (*Send.*) Same… shit emoji… Every few days. (*Send.*)

C   Typing… Typing… Typing…

E   Boss just showed me the meme going around. (*Send.*)

D   Which one? (*Send.*)

A   'PM watching words leave his mouth' meme. (*Send.*)

E   Search GIF: 'Pretending to laugh.' Delete. Search GIF: 'Laughs in British.' (*Send.*)

A   Search GIF: 'Not impressed eyeroll.' (*Send.*)

C   Typing... Typing... Typing...

D   Funny meme. But pretty sure he knew what he was doing. (*Send*.)

B   Tempted to have second breakfast. (*Send*.)

A   (*Voice-note recording*.) 'My colleague just said that the PM was obviously wrong but put it down to his *quirky* character.' (*Send*.)

E   Face-palm emoji. Quirky. Yeah. Right. (*Send*.)

D   This isn't a quirk. This is his *normal*. (*Send*.)

B   Depressing conversation. Tired-face emoji. Give Netflix suggestions. (*Send*.)

E   What the duck is *normal* anyway? (*Send*.)

B   Search GIF: 'Film reel.' (*Send*.)

C   Typing... Typing... Typing...

A   *This* right? This is the 'new' *normal*. PM talks. Search GIF: 'Chaos grenade.' (*Send*.) PM walks away. *Normal*. (*Send*.)

B   Search GIF: 'Eats popcorn.' (*Send*.)

D   Been like this forever. We're just talking about it more now. (*Send*.)

E   So, new *normal* is actually *old* normal. Thumbs-up emoji! (*Send*.)

D   Real question should be. Whose 'normal' are we talking about? (*Send*.)

A   Search GIF: 'True story.' (*Send*.)

B   Is it *normal* that I bought another breakfast from the canteen but pretended it was for my boss? (*Send*.)

A   News update. Press release from PM on way. (*Send*.)

E   Great. Can't wait. #SorryNotSorry. (*Send*.)

A   Optimistic. To think it will say sorry at all. (*Send*.)

E   Angry-face emoji. (*Send*.) Feel like uninstalling all news apps. (*Send*.)

D   Do it. I uninstall all the time. Less noisy. (*Send*.)

C   Typing... Typing... Typing...

A   Search GIF: 'Tempting.' (*Send*.) Less noisy. Alright. Going to try. (*Send*.)

B   Me too. (*Send*.)

E   Pass. Need to know what's going on. (*Send*.)

D   (*Voice-note recording*.) 'You can still find out what's going on guys. Without the constant updates.' (*Send*.)

A   I've done it! (*Send*.)

B   Me too! (*Send*.)

E   Now I've got FOMO! (*Send*.)

B   Search GIF: 'Just do it.' (*Send*.)

E   Search GIF: 'Giving in to peer pressure.' (*Send*.)
     ...Done! #BitWeird. (*Send*.)

A   Search GIF: 'Back to work.' (*Send*.)

C   Lol @ '*PM watching words leave his mouth*.' (*Send*.)

B   'Why do you always join the chat an hour later?! The conversation has moved on!' (*Send*.)

C   Gasp (*Send*.) Search GIF: 'Rude!' (*Send*.)

DIFFERENT

Characters: A (*female*), B (*male*).

News plays on low volume in the background.

A   Last night was fun. I knew you'd get along with them all. They *loved* you. The messages on the group chat this morning! You have a fan club.

B   That's nice.

A   I shouldn't tell you this, but they all said that you're *exactly* the kind of guy they've always pictured me with. I mean, I think they meant 'end-up-with'. But I told them. We've only been together six months. It's not exactly the time to talk about 'end-up-with'.

　　　Beat.

　　　Is it?

B   No. It's not.

A   Right. Yeah. That's what I said... Anyway, I'm glad you finally got to meet everyone. I know you'd met most of them, but it was nice to meet them all together... It's only lunchtime, and I'm already exhausted. I don't know how I'm going to get through this Zoom meeting. You have a call too, right?

B   Yes. Soon.

A   Okay, I'm going to eat at my desk. I've made a salad, and there's an extra sandwich in / the –

B   – What / did they mean?

A   What?

B   Your friends. What did they mean?

A   When?

B   At the end of the night.

A   What did they say?

B   That... in your '*predictable-unpredictableness*', I'm obviously someone you would... *choose* to be with.

A   Oh, they were being silly. Nothing to read into.

B   I know. I'd still like to know though. What did they
        mean exactly? Why am I *obviously* someone you would
        choose to be with?

A   I don't know.

        Beat.

B   You *do*.

A   Well, I guess they meant someone with your good
        qualities.

B   Okay... But what about me specifically?

A   *Specifically?*

B   Exactly. *Specifically.* They've known, however many of,
        your past boyfriends. Did they ever say the same about
        them?

A   Well, no... I didn't realise it's a problem.

B   What is?

A   That I've dated lots of men.

B   It's not.

A   That's not what it sounds like to me. '*However many
        of...*'

B   No, no. I'm not one of / those...

A   Because I've dated. And I'm not ashamed of it. I've
        dated all kinds of different men.

B   *Different!* Yes. *That.*

A   What?

B   '*Different.*' What does it mean?

A   I don't understand.

B   Last night they were asking me *so* many questions.

A   I thought that was a good thing?

B   It is. It is.

A   What's wrong then?

B   '*Different*.'

A   …

B   You described me as '*different*'.

A   When?

B   When they were asking about my history. My faith. You said, '*Yes, but he's different*'. What does 'different' mean? In the context of my faith.

A   I don't remember saying it.

B   You don't? But you *must* remember *feeling* it. At some point. Because you *did* say it. So, that must mean you have *felt* it. And *thought* it.

A   I honestly don't know. I don't see you as… I mean. You're *you*.

B   *Different?*

A   Yes. No! Look, stop twisting my words.

B   I haven't twisted your words. I've literally said what you said to them. I've repeated it back to you. And I'm simply trying to determine what makes me 'different' to say, some of my friends or family members.

A   Well, they're different too.

B   In what way exactly?

A   All I mean is that none of you are what most people expect.

B   What do *most* people expect?

A   You know. You're not *practising*.

B   So?

A   That's what you think. Someone who *practises* the faith.

B   Some of my friends and family practise. Some *don't*. Some *do* depending on the time of year. Others don't.

So, what are they *different* to exactly? Because the only ones you know are through *me*.

A   That's not true.

B   Isn't it? Who else is there?

A   At work.

B   Are they '*different*' too?

A   Okay, no. I'm not having this. This *accusation* you're trying to throw at me. Without saying it directly.

B   You'd rather I said it *directly*?

A   You know how much work I do in this area, right? I've already told you. I've even got myself a reputation in the office. Because I call people out. People who *think* like *that*. I've arranged *talks* about this subject. About offensive language. The *harm* it can do.

B   I *thank* you for it.

A   I'm not looking for *thanks*.

B   Aren't you?

A   That's what you think of me?

B   No. I don't think anything. Or I didn't until yesterday. When you said I was '*different*'.

A   Fucking hell. I can't believe you're doing this right now...

B   All I want is for you to *say* what you *mean*...

A   ...You're asking me all these questions...

B   ...I don't want you to hide behind words you *think* are complimentary.

A   ...I have a *meeting*. And I *need* to prepare.

B   I *need* to know what you think I'm '*different*' from.

A   Nothing! No one, okay! It was a slip of the tongue.

B   But you've been trying to *explain* it! You *still* believe it. So, tell me straight. What does it mean...? *What does it mean?*

A   Nothing! Okay. Nothing!

B   It means *something*! So, *say* it. *Just* say it!

A   You're not a *fucking* – !

      Pause.

B   Right. Right... *Thank you.*

      B *walks off.*

SEE IT SAY IT

Characters: A, B.

A   So, if I *see* something… I *say* it?

B   Yes.

A   And then it's *sorted*?

B   Yes. Then it's sorted.

A   Okay…

B   Okay?

A   Great.

B   Great.

     Beat.

A   What exactly though?

B   What *exactly*?

A   It will help to have… *specifics*.

     Beat.

B   Well, things that are a little… 'different'.

A   '*Different*'?

B   Yes, '*different*'.

A   Okay…

B   Got it?

A   Got it.

B   Great.

A   Great!

     Beat.

     What does 'different' mean though?

B   What does it *mean*?

A   Again, specifics would be helpful.

     Beat.

B   Anything that isn't… 'normal'.

A   Okay. Not '*normal*'?

B   Yes. Not '*normal*'.

A   Right…

B   Got it?

A   Got it.

B   Great.

A   Great!

Beat.

What exactly is '*normal*' though?

B   What '*exactly*'?

A   …

B   You *know*…

A   …

B   …

A   …Feels a bit weird saying it.

B   There's no one else here.

Beat.

A   I know…

Beat.

B   Why don't you look it up?

A   Look it up? Okay…

B   Okay?

A   Great.

B   Great!

A *searches on phone.*

A   'Normal. *Adjective*. Conforming to a standard, regular pattern. Something that is *usual*. Typical. Expected. *Not* strange…' Ah, okay!

B   Okay?

A   Okay!

B   Great!

A   Great!

     A *looks at phone again*.

     Oh, wait. There's a technical definition. Mathematical…

B   I don't think you need to know –

A   – 'An imaginary line forming a *right*-angle with the tangent to a *curved* surface at a *particular* point.'

     Beat.

B   Did that help you at all?

A   Not really, no.

B   Look, it's straightforward. Keep an eye out for anything that looks '*suspicious*'.

A   '*Suspicious*'?

B   '*Suspicious*.' Things that aren't '*normal*'.

A   Okay. Not normal. '*Suspicious*.'

B   Yes.

A   So, if it's *not* '*normal*' it's '*suspicious*'?

B   Yes. I mean. Kind of… You <u>know</u>.

A   …

B   Well, we all know what '*normal*' is.

A   Right. Okay. So, because we know what '*normal*' is, we know what '*suspicious*' is.

B   Exactly. Recognise the '*normal*' and then the '*suspicious*' will show itself. Naturally. Got it?

A   Yes, absolutely! Got! It!

B   Great?

A   *Great!*

      Beat.

B   Don't *overthink* it.

A   Okay. Perfect!

      Pause.

      But what about –

B   – Oh, for god's sake! You know what '*normal*' is. We *all*
      know what '*normal*' is. I know it. You know it. *They*
      know it. Don't make me *say* it. You'll know it when you
      see it. You'll know 'normal'. And *therefore* you'll know
      '*different*'. A difference. Something that differs from
      normal. Sometimes *openly*. Sometimes *discreetly*.
      Things that are *dissimilar* from normal. And therefore
      suspicious. And it's *different* we want to –

A   – *Prevent?*

B   Yes.

A   And that's the strategy?

B   No.

A   No?

B   That's the *duty*.

PAUSES.

Characters: A, B.

A   Okay, let me get this straight...

B   Sure.

A   ...Despite doing all the research, reading, talking to experts, and *even* writing the literature review... you want to now *scrap* your dissertation topic, and start again?

B   Yes.

A   So, instead of writing about...

B   First language acquisition.

A   You want to...

B   Explore what language does in the body.

A   When it...?

B   Pauses. Stops. Hesitates. *Has* to police itself.

A   As opposed to?

B   When language flows freely. Like a river. When it doesn't stop. When it doesn't *have* to stop. Or pause. When it can escape the tongue *from* the brain without *pausing*. When it doesn't damage organs or skin because it's trapped in the body. And what happens to *those* who have to swallow their words. Where do those words *sit*? *In* the body I mean.

     Beat.

A   And then what?

B   I'll propose finding little spaces. *Soundless* spaces. In the body. Where words can *escape* without anyone knowing. *Maybe* even without *us* knowing. Then we don't have to feel them *stuck* somewhere. And so, there's no more pain or cracks or crunches or breaks or snaps or fractures or sounds of gnawing as we try to release them. From the *body*, I mean. Then maybe we can stop the *onslaught*. Of damaged bodies.

THE WEDGE

Characters: A (*male*), B (*male*), C.

A   As a *follower* of the faith –

B   – *So* am I…

A   I say the Prime Minister's comments are simply a reflection of this country's *perceptions*. A reality we *must* acknowledge and are not… '*that*'!

B   I *disagree*. *If* we are to *deal* with this *issue*, then we *must* call it *exactly* what it *is*. Which is a '*Phobia*'.

A   As a *member* of the faith –

B   – So am *I*…

A   Calling it… '*that*'… stops legitimate criticisms of the faith.

B   No, calling it a '*Phobia*' reflects the accurate *feeling* of *offence* being directed *at*, and *therefore*, being *felt* by the *actual* community.

C   So, does the community actually *agree* that this is, *in fact*, a '*Phobia*'?

A   No.

B   Yes.

A   No!

B   Yes! As one of the many individuals of the faith –

A   – *I am also!*

B   We won't *all* agree on the same things.

A   I *agree* with that. And as I *am* an *adherent* of the faith…

B   – *I am too!*

A   …

     Beat.

C   Were you going to add to that?

A   No.

C   Okay. Why is it *this* difficult to *define* and *agree* on a *word*?

A   Because this is as *tough* and as *complicated* as trying to *define* a potato.

     Beat.

C   …What do you mean?

A   Well, we must first acknowledge that there are different *kinds* of potatoes. And then we must ask ourselves: what exactly *is* a potato? Are there *good* potatoes and *bad* potatoes? *Yes.* Are *all* potatoes the same? *No.* There are russet potatoes. White potatoes. Fingerling potatoes. And even *petit* potatoes…

B   You mean baby potatoes…?

A   …And we *must* go further. Does everyone like potatoes? No. Do we still *eat* them? *Probably.* They *are* good for you. But not too much. There are a lot of carbs.

C   What are you saying?

A   I don't know. But in this analogy, I am a *potato*. And I am *not* offended.

HE KNEW ME

Characters: A, B (*female*).

A   Can you tell me what happened first?

B   He *punched* the window.

A   When?

B   When he saw me.

A   When he *saw* you?

B   Yes.

A   Did you know him?

B   No. He was a stranger. He *is* a stranger. To me.

A   And *you* a stranger to him?

B   No.

A   No?

B   I couldn't have been.

A   Why?

B   No one gets this angered by a stranger. A *stranger* they saw getting onto the bus.

A   I don't understand. Had you *seen* him before?

B   No.

A   But he had seen *you* before?

B   *Yes*.

A   Where?

B   Everywhere.

A   What do you mean *everywhere*?

B   There was *so* much anger. I expected it to *pour* out of him. Like a river. Like a *river* trying to *escape* his body. But it didn't. It was *just* blood.

A   *Where* had you seen him before?

B *Nowhere*.

A Then how had *he*… I can't make sense of this until you tell me *clearly*.

B I *am* telling you clearly.

A *What* are you *telling* me?

B I'm telling you that I didn't know *him* but *he* knew *me*! He *saw* me and he *knew* me… Images. Shows. Headlines. Videos. Scrolling. Front pages. Words. Clothes. Symbols. Skin. *Colour*. He knew me *intimately*. *Even* if he'd *never* seen *me* before. And *I* had *never* seen *him* before. He still *knew* me. He *thought* he knew me. And so, he got angry. He saw me and *he* got *angry*. And he punched the window. Because *everything* about *me* made him angry. And in that situation, I'd never be able to tell him otherwise. Because, he *knows* me… Doesn't he?

NORMAL 2 – LATE AFTERNOON

Characters: A, B, C, D, E.

WhatsApp scene. This scene can be played as simply words being said in a group.

A   #BetterMood. (*Send.*)

B   Me too. Also, eating less. (*Send.*)

E   Keep checking for the news apps. #BadHabit. (*Send.*)

D   You'll get used to it. (*Send.*)

A   Good to be connected. But also. This reminds me of simpler times. (*Send.*)

B   Search GIF: 'True that.' (*Send.*)

D   Like riding bikes as kids. (*Send.*)

E   Hanging with cousins. (*Send.*)

C   Search GIF: 'Playing games.' (*Send.*)

B   Oh, you joined the conversation at the right moment this time! (*Send.*)

C   Search GIF: 'Piss Off.' (*Send.*)

B   Search GIF: 'LMAO!' (*Send.*)

D   (*Voice-note recording.*) 'Did anyone play that game as kids? Lists? Under certain topics.' (*Send.*)

A   Names, places, animals, et cetera? (*Send.*)

D   Yes, that one! (*Send.*)

B   Yes! And we used to fight about whether words in our mother tongue instead of English was cheating.

D   More fun playing for bilinguals! (*Send.*)

B   Search GIF: 'The drama!' (*Send.*)

E   Search GIF: 'The nostalgia.' (*Send.*)

B   I miss those things. (*Send.*)

C   All the good things. (*Send.*)

A   The beautiful things. (*Send.*)

E   Our things. (*Send.*)

C   Our normal! (*Send.*)

E   – Our normal…? (*Send.*)

WONDERFUL COUNTRY

Characters: A, B.

A *and* B *sitting next to each other, watching TV.*

A   They're saying this is a wonderful country…

B   It is. Wonderful.

A   So wonderful.

B   So, *so* wonderful.

      Beat.

A   S*uch* a wonderful country.

B   A *wonderful* country.

A   *Really* wonderful.

B   Really, *really* wonderful.

      Beat.

A   Wonderful. Like cake.

B   And tea.

A   Wonderful like cake and tea.

      Beat.

B   Sometimes –

A   – Sometimes it's even *more* wonderful.

B   Absolutely. So *much* more wonderful.

A   Flowing with wonderfulness.

B   Yes. Flowing *full* of wonderfulness.

      Beat.

B   But sometimes –

A   – *Sometimes* it's even *more* bloody wonderful.

B   I *agree*. More wonderful.

A   That's right. *More* wonderful.

B   A *more* wonderful, *wonderful* country.

        Beat.

        It's *just* that *sometimes* –

A   – Sometimes it's *fucking* wonderful! Okay? *They* say it's wonderful. It's *wonderful*! *Bloody* wonderful. Wonder-*bloody*-full!

B   Okay! It's wonderful!

A   *Bloody* wonderful!

B   Bloody *wonderful*!

A   Wonder-*bloody*-full!

B   Full-bloody-*wonderful*!

A   *Bloody, bloody* wonderful!

B   *Bloody, bloody, bloody* wonderful!

A/B   Wonderful! It's wonderful! *Bloody, bloody, bloody* wonderful! Wonderful! *Bloody, bloody, bloody, bloody* wonderful! So wonderful! So *bloody* wonderful! Full of wonderful! *Bloody* wonderfulness! Wonderful, wonderful, *bloody wonderfullllllll*!

I CONDEMN

Characters: A, B.

A   The thing is…

B   I understand.

A   You *understand*?

B   *I* understand.

A   So, you understand that you *must*? Because they *could*…

B   I *must*. And I *do*.

A   And you *mean* it?

B   With *every* part of me.

       Beat.

A   So, this time, did you –

B   – I did. I condemned.

A   And did you…

B   I criticised.

A   You did?

B   Yes.

A   How many times?

B   Every time.

A   And did you…

B   I explained. I *tried* to explain.

A   But you know there are *no* explanations, *right*?

B   Yes. I explained that there are *no* explanations.

       Beat.

A   Were you angry enough?

B   I cursed.

A   How many times?

B   *Every* time.

A   And did you…

B   Yes. I took to the streets.

A   In what weather?

B   In the freezing weather. *And* the scorching-hot weather.
      Even when no one saw me.

A   They do *need* to see you though. Otherwise, they don't
      know whose side you are on.

B   I know.

      Beat.

A   Did they at least *hear* you?

B   I can't know that.

A   You *must* know how important it is?

B   I can only *do* what I can *do*.

A   *That's* the wrong answer.

B   I know.

      Beat.

A   So, what will you do *next* time?

B   I'll hope there *isn't* a next time.

A   But *if* there is?

B   I'll do it all over again. So they would *know*.
      I'll denounce.
      I'll renounce.
      I'll decry.
      I'll cry.
      I'll *pause* and *hide*.
      I'll reject and disown.
      I'll turn *away* from my *own*.
      I'll stop thinking *and*,
      I'll think too much.
      I'll *hide* in plain sight.

I'll *memorise*.
I'll *trivialise*.
I'll *subject and* be *made* a subject.
I'll *condemn*...
I'll apologise.
I'll berate.
I'll beg.
I'll attack.
I'll *lambaste*.
I'll disparage.
I'll denigrate.
I'll *vilify*.
I'll malign.
I'll reprehend.
I'll *discredit*.
I'll revile.
I'll *reject*.
I'll denunciate.
I'll *shout* when my voice is lost.
I'll *shout*.
I'll *scream* and *shout*.
I'll do it *all*
For them.
To them.
And they will *know*!
I'm on their side.

Beat.

I'll *swear* it. I'm on *their* side.

HARES

Characters: A, B.

Each holds a suntanning reflector.

A   Boss made a *boo-boo* again.

B   Boo-boo.

A   Journos asking for comments *all* day.

B   Journos. *Gross.*

A   Want to know if I *agree* with him. Or if I'll *defend 'The Community'.*

B   LOL. The *'Community'.*

A   Wish I could tell them *straight.* I have more in common with *Hares* than *'The Community'*…

B   Yes! *Hares.*

A   …And *'The Community'* is more like rabbits.

B   Rabbits. *Nom, nom.*

A   I have a *different* community, thank you very much.

B   Thank you *very* much.

A   The *Hare* Community.

B   Hares. Yay!

A   We *Hares* are *very* different.

B   *Different.* Thank you very much.

A   And *The Rabbits* are… *disgusting.*

B   *Disgusting!*

A   *They* live underground. But *we Hares* live above.

B   Above!

A   *They* crowd with their *own.* Whilst *we* live *alone.*

B   Alone!

A   We *Hares* are faster…

B   Faster!

A   Stronger…

B   Stronger!

A   We are the *best* there is!

B   *Best* there is!

A   And the *best* there *ever* will be!

B   *The best!*

A   *The best, best, best!*

B   *Meow…!*

A   *Meow…!*

       A *and* B *both make meow noises.*

BAD FATHER

Characters: A, B (*male*).

A   You haven't been well?

B   No.

A   Do you *recognise* that you're not well?

B   Yes.

A   Did someone point it out?

B   Yes.

A   Who?

B   My father.

A   Your *father*? What did he say?

B   That I'm not well.

A   Did you know that already? *Before* he said it?

B   I felt it. But I didn't *know* it.

A   How do you think *he* knew it?

B   Because he was also unwell. *Once*.

A   Did he tell you that?

B   Yes. And he said that one day, I will see my *own* sons unwell. And I will know it before they do.

A   So, you're a father? *Now?*

B   Yes. But not a good one.

A   You're not a good father?

B   I'm *not* a good father.

A   Why?

B   I didn't prepare them. My sons.

A   For what?

B   For the world. I wanted to do things *differently* to *my* father.

A In what way?

B My father told me that the world is a bad place. And you *must* be ready for it.

A And what did you tell your sons?

B I told them the world is a *good* place.

A And that's *not* what your father told you?

B No. He told me that the world is *cruel*.

A And you didn't believe him?

B I know the world wasn't good to him. Or *even* to me. But I believed it *could* be better. I believed it *was* better. *Now*.

  Beat.

A Why did you want it to be better?

B I didn't want my sons to hide away. My father taught me to be *small*. I wanted to teach my sons to be *tall*. I'm a bad father.

A How did you do that? How did you teach your sons to be tall?

B '*Sticks and stones*.'

A Sticks and stones?

B 'Sticks and stones may break my bones. But words will never hurt me.' I taught them. *Every* night. After work. When I got home. '*Sticks and stones may break your bones but words will never hurt you*.' I taught them over and over and *over* again. And they believe it. They believe it in *every* part of them...

  Beat.

  I'm a *bad* father.

A Why does that make you a bad father?

B Because they'll hear *words*. The *words* my father heard once. The *words* I heard once. The *words* I heard once *again. Today. And* yesterday. The same words. The *same* words. And they'll think about what I taught them. '*Sticks and stones may break your bones but words will never hurt you.*' And they'll *know* that *I* was *wrong*. And that I'm a *bad* father.

A   Isn't it true? That sticks and stones can break your bones but words will never *hurt* you?

B   No, it's a lie. A *complete* lie. Because the world isn't *better*. I prepared them wrong. And you know what? Words don't always land on your body and fall off. They *hit* you like *artillery* fire. They *seep* into your *bones*. They *shatter* your bones. I should have told them *that*. '*Sticks and stones may break your bones but words will shatter you!*' Like glass.

Beat.

A   Where are your sons now?

B   With my father. I told my father to hide them away. I told him to *cover* their ears. Like he covered *mine*. I told him to *prepare* my sons. Because he was *right*. And I'm a *bad* father.

MOTHER TONGUE

Characters: A (*female*), B (*female*).

A   I have no idea *how*, or *where* it came from. It was *so* weird!

B   I know...

A   Has it happened to you?

B   *Yes*. Sometimes even when I do crossword puzzles.

A   That's *better* than in a work meeting!

B   I know, I know... But it still catches me off-guard... You know, I remember my ama asked me once, 'Do you *think* in English?' I'd never even given it a thought. I *do* think in English... But when it *does* happen. Like it did with *you* today. When a *word* from my mother tongue appears *before* the English word for the same thing... I love it. It's like, even if I don't *think* in it, the words have clearly been floating around peacefully in my body. As if they're bubbles ready to *burst* when they want to... And then, it always makes me think about how one day, when we *all* have our *own* children. We'll blow those same bubbles into their palms. And watch them gently *dissolve* and *dissipate* into their bodies. And how *that* will be *our* gift to them. Like the *gift* our mothers gave us. Because *sometimes* the *only* way to *feel* is in your mother tongue... Does that make *sense*?

A   Yeah... It *really* does.

THEATRE

Characters: A, B, C.

A   Staging looks great.

B   Yes, looks *great*.

C   *Really* good.

A   *Such* an important topic.

B   Really is.

C   *Very* important.

A   Especially today.

B   *Especially.*

C   *Definitely* today.

       Beat.

A   His press team must be having a *nightmare* day. *Unbelievable* really. That anyone could be *so...* Whatever the word is.

C   *Yes.*

B   *Whatever* the word is.

       Beat.

A   In light of that, *this* is an important topic. *In* this play.

B   Yes.

C   *So* important.

       Beat.

A   Someone in the ticket queue was talking about it too.

B   Saying?

C   Yes, *saying*?

A   That it was a *terrible* thing to say.

B   *So* terrible.

C   *Really* terrible.

    Beat.

A   I try to stay out of the conversations about this kind of thing.

B   Me too.

C   *Same.*

    Beat.

A   Problem is that people expect me to have an opinion.

B   Oh, me too!

C   Every time!

    Beat.

A   But if I'm *honest. At least* with you both.

B   Oh, only *us* three.

C   *Threesome* secrets!

A   *Sometimes* you have to look at *why* these things are said.

B   Oh, *absolutely.*

C   *I* agree.

A   The *community really* needs to try harder.

B   Absolutely!

C   Agreed!

A   I mean, look at *us*. We go to the *theatre*.

B   *Here* we are…

C   *In* the theatre!

A   We prioritise *fitting* in.

B   *Exactly.*

C   Yes!

A   *And* learning.

B   Education.

C   *A-B-C*, motherfuckers.

A   It's simple really. If you *try*…

B   If you *really* try…

A   Oh, show's about to start.

B   Oh, yes!

C   …E-F-G.

        Beat.

A   This ice cream is *nice*.

B   *Very* nice.

C   *Great!*

A   What flavour did everyone get?

A/B/C *Vanilla*.

PASS THE SALT

Characters: A (*male*), B (*female*), C (*female*), D (*male*).

A   They're late…

B   (*Offstage.*) They're probably stuck in traffic.

A   I don't understand why traffic is so *significantly* bad
      when it rains. I've never understood that.

B   (*Offstage.*) People are more cautious. Everyone drives
      slower.

A   But it's a *disproportionate* amount of traffic. I *understand*
      traffic increases. But I'll never understand *why* it increases
      this much. Like last week. It took *fifty minutes* to drive to
      your mother's. When, usually, when the weather is fine, it
      takes twenty minutes. *Fifteen* even. *Three times* longer!

      Knock on door.

      They're here…

      C *and* D *enter.*

C   Sorry we're late.

A   Not late at all. Come in. Welcome… *Honey*, they're
      here!

B   (*Offstage.*) Coming!

D   Cats and dogs outside… Something smells *good*.

A   You're in for a treat.

      B *enters.*

B   Sorry. Couldn't find my shoes.

A   You look beautiful, sweetheart.

C   Apologies about the time. *Horrendous* traffic.

A   How long were you stuck in traffic?

C   Um, twenty, twenty-five minutes…?

D   Yeah, about that much.

A That proves my point. They live a ten-minute drive away, but they were stuck in traffic for *double* the amount of time.

C I think we've missed something...

B He's on one of his traffic rants again.

D Oh, right!

B But I *think* we can stop talking about traffic now.

D *And* weather!

C Yes, those are for when the conversation *really* starts to wane.

D So long as we avoid *politics*, we're safe.

B Agreed!

A Oh, come on! The party starts when politics are introduced into the mix. *Especially* with a martini in your hand...?

C I won't say no to a *martini*.

D Martini *minus* the politics for me, please... What's on the menu tonight? It smells *incredible*.

B Not my doing this time. *He's* the chef tonight.

A My own twist on a good old Indian her mother taught me.

B Bengali...

D *You* cooked it?

C Hold on, is that even *legitimate*?

B It's a Bengali dish...

A *Wait* until you try it.

B ...Not Indian.

A Of course. I apologise.

D Has he made it before or are *we* the guinea pigs?

A   A number of times. *And* I've perfected it…

C   Setting expectations *quite* high then.

A   …Right, darling?

B   I've told him to add more salt. He *always* skimps on the salt.

A   It's not good for you.

B   Well, let's make sure there's salt on the table please…

A   Anyway, I put *roughly* the same amount her mother does.

B   Doesn't taste *quite* like my mother's… But I *must* say, it's not bad.

A   That's good enough for me!

D   How is your mother?

B   Doing well now… Thank you.

C   What happened to your mother?

B   She had a little fall. Nothing serious. She's better now.

A   Not *completely* better though. She's insisting on moving *back* to Bangladesh.

B   Oh, can we not…

A   She's been saying it for a while but since her fall, she's *really* ramped it up.

D   Does she have anyone there?

B   Some relatives. But I'd rather she was here, where I can check in on her myself.

C   Why does she want to move back?

A   That's a *good* question. With a *very* silly answer.

B   It's not silly…

A   She *thinks* we're all going to be kicked out of the country!

C   '*We*'?

A   Okay, not '*we*'.

B   She's old, and she worries.

D   Why does she think that?

B   Let's not get into this now.

A   She *thinks* this country has become *racist* again. And that the government is going to *ship out* all the minorities.

D   She doesn't?... That's incredibly sad.

A   That's one way of looking at it... Shall we sit down?

B   Did you bring the salt?

C   You can see why she said it though. I mean, I don't believe it will happen, but you can see *where* that fear would stem from.

D   Oh, no! No politics at the dinner table.

B   I agree!

C   If the Prime Minister is saying things like he *did* today...

A   Look, I'm no fan of the man. But you *get* where he's coming from.

B   Honey, you didn't bring the salt.

C   '*Get where he's coming from*'?! It was incredibly racist.

A   'Racist' is a bit of a strong word.

D   I agree. Offensive maybe, but not racist... That's *all* I'm going to say on the matter.

A   It's offensive if you *choose* to be offended.

B   Honey, the *salt*.

A   I'll get it...

C   (*To* B.) What's your view on all this?

B   I try not to talk about politics. It's safer for our marriage!

A   He *clearly* meant that it can be '*seen*' that way.

B   You've got the salt?

A   Yes… Which is a *fact*, by the way. People *do* see it as that.

C   Because of the one-sided stories they're fed.

        (*To* B.) Don't you think?

B   I'd rather go back to talking about traffic…

D   …Hear, hear!

A   Maybe. But my point is that it *is* a *fact*. People *do see* it in that way. And I don't understand why he's being *penalised* for stating a *fact*.

C   Well, he didn't *state* it as a researched *or* scientific *fact*. He stated it as a *personal* opinion.

D   This martini is good.

A   I disagree.

B   Pass the salt down the table please.

C   And if it *is,* indeed, a '*fact*' then surely her mother's right to feel the way she does.

B   Honey, the salt…

A   How's that?

C   If so many believe what he said to be a *fact,* then she is legitimate in feeling *scared* by them *thinking* it.

B   I need the salt…

A   But it's also a fact that the threat is coming from *their* side.

C   '*Their*'?

B   *Please*.

D   Hm, yummy martini.

A   As in the *other* side. It's a fact that so many people *think* it, but it's also a *fact* that it has *elements* of the truth.

B   *Salt*. Please.

C So, what you're saying is that *her* mother is more of a *threat* than the rest of society because she follows a particular belief system?

D Quite hungry now.

A We are talking about the *collective*. *Not* individuals.

C (*To* B.) What do you think?

B I just need the *salt*.

A She doesn't like talking about it. We've clashed in the past, but the reality is that she's *renounced* it.

B No, I haven't.

A Well, you've renounced your mother's '*conservative version*'.

B I don't think of it as a '*version*'.

A Whatever the right word is.

C Hold on. Hold on... Her mother *taught* you *this* dish, right?

D It smells good...

B It *needs* salt.

C So, what difference does it make what '*version*' she follows? You get along. And her faith is her faith.

B *Please* pass the salt down...

A My point is that it took for *me* to marry her daughter for *her* mother to become more open. *Even* if she still holds on to most of the conservative parts. She *had to* adjust her views...

B Pass the salt. *Please*.

A ...Otherwise she may *never* have.

B (*Shouts*.) PASS THE SALT!

 Silence.

You assume the salt is *fine*. You *assume* that my
tastebuds won't be *offended* by the lack of salt in the
food, *or* the *lack* of salt on the *table*. In the *food* that *my*
mother taught *you* to make. You assume that *your* idea of
the right amount of salt is *correct*. It's measured by *you,*
and the food *you're* used to eating. Even though this is a
dish that *my ama* taught *you* to make. And she *always*
uses more salt. You assume because I *now* eat amongst
you, that I like the same amount of salt as you. Well, I
don't. So, for the last time. Please, *please*, can you pass
me THE FUCKING SALT!

BREXIT

Characters: A (*male*), B (*male*).

A   This is a moment.

B   It *is* a moment.

A   A moment to remember –

B   – A moment *to* remember.

A   Will it be?

B   What?

A   Remembered.

B   It should be –

A   – *Should?*

B   It *could* be.

    Beat.

A   And how do we ensure that happens?

B   We *find* it a name.

A   A *name*…?

B   A *name* that makes it a considerable moment *in* history…

A   'Rivers of Blood'…

B   '*Believe* in Britain.'

A   'Take Back *Control*'…

B   'We Want *Our* Country *Back*!'

    Beat.

    A *name* that turns and spins. Changes directions… Continues to be *heard* and *seen* in the future by *every* generation.

A   Buses…

B   Newspapers.

A   Images…

B   Viral!… We make it a Tower of Babel until it isn't…
      Give it a name that brings *all* our own *together* until it
      can lock the door behind it. Britain will *leave*…

A   *And exit*.

A/B   *Brexit!*

BONES

Characters: A.

A   He won't resign. No one will expect him to. It's *okay* to say things like that now. A few people will call him out on it. And then… we move on.

Or at least some people do. Rest of us are trying not to fall completely through the cracks.

Or maybe we're trying to get *through* the cracks into a bigger space. I can't define that space. But a space where I'm allowed to… *exist*.

What do I mean? Fuck knows.

But the thing is, I feel down *all* the time. And I'm not sure why.

No, not about the state of the world. Yes, the last few years. We've *all* been worried about that…

…I've become conscious that my sadness has become harder to hide. I *always* want to keep a mask on.

Why am I sad? No, it's not what he said. Maybe it should be. But it's not.

I am just sad. And I don't know why.

Sadness is sitting in my belly. It is sucking up the food and nutrients. And I'm trying to take crumbs from life to keep me going.

No, not what he *said*. I mean yeah, it's not okay. Of course it's not. But it's not that. Can be. Maybe. Seen. As *that*. For me. Making me. I don't. Making me. Think. Sad. *I don't*.

…

I *can't* describe. I *don't* have the.

I just know that every rib has been *cracking* slowly for a long time.

Maybe I felt less *cracked* yesterday than I do today.

No, how could it be because of what he *said*! Words don't crack bones…

...Do they?

Sticks and stones and all that.

I simply know that I'm *cracking*. Slowly. But *constantly*. Crack. Cracking.

I can't show those cracks to anyone. I *feel* they'll crumble.

Do you know what a face looks like when it's hiding *cracks* cracking inside the body? My father had that face. The face of a *cracked* man...

That word sounds painful, doesn't it? Crack. Cracked. *Cracking*.

There are words that *sound* how they sound. I remember learning that in English.

The word '*crack*' sounds like a *crack*.

And that's why you *hide* your *cracks*. I don't think people would be able to *bear* that sound if we let them hear it.

You know, there's a *crack* coming from us *so* often, I wonder how we stand.

Ribs and bones *crack*. I wish they *dissolved* instead. And we could throw them out. Our tongues *spitting* them out.

But bones *don't* dissolve. They *crack*.

Old cracks. *New* cracks. Bones *waiting to be* cracked.

Maybe it could be its *own* language. Right?

Each *crack*. A crack, if it could be *heard,* would spell out different words.

Crack *A*.
Crack *B*.
Crack *C*.
Crack *D*.
Crack *E*.
Crack *F*.
Crack *Aliph*

Bay
Pay
tay
Tay
Thay
Seh
Jeem
Chay
Hay
Alif
Baa
Taa
Tha
Jiim
Haa
Khaa
Alif
Ba
Ta
Jeem
Xa
Kha
Deel
Ra
Siin
Alef
Be
Pe
Te
Se
Jim
Ce
He

They wouldn't sound the same...

Beat.

...A *crack* until there are no more *cracks*.
Because there are no more *bones* left.
To crack.

No more.

NO. 10 PRESS OFFICE

11 P.M.

Characters: A, B, C, D, E.

A, B, C, D *on stage*.

D   'With *still* no apology *or* statement from the Prime Minister's Office, despite officials in China, India, US *and* France lending him their approval, and even *here*, in the UK, conservative and far-right groups praising his use of words, we must once again ask ourselves... is this Prime Minister still fit to govern a *United* Kingdom?'

B   Lefty nonsense!

A   As if he'd resign over something like *this*.

B   His position is solid.

A   *Exactly*.

B   It'd take a bloody coup to remove him.

     D*'s phone beeps*.

A   Tell me he's on his way back?

D   He's finishing his pint whilst he waits for it to stop raining.

B   Fucking hell.

     E *arrives*.

E   Updates?

D   Your contact stepped up.

B   Other news has pushed the story down.

D   But not massively.

C   We've posted lots of pictures of him holding cats...

B   *And* interacting with community members.

C   ...But the cat ones are more popular.

A   The story *still* isn't dying though...

E   Keep an eye on the polls.

        D's phone beeps.

D   Okay. He's making his way back.

B   Finally!

D   But he wants us to make sure he isn't *hounded* by press
        questions on arrival.

B   Of course they're going to hound him!

D   He *feels* he's answered all the questions he *needs* to.

A   He's been answering *questions* with *other* questions
        all day!

B   And quoting out-of-context Shakespeare and Churchill
        to everyone!

A   We *need* him to apologise now!

B   He won't apologise, so *stop* making that suggestion!

D   He was *really* clear about that.

A   Look at the state of all this! How else are we supposed to
        clear this shit up?!

        They argue over each other. Until –

C   He's gone up.

B   Gone up?

C   His rating.

A   I thought you were making notes…

C   Sorry. Got distracted.

E   How much?

        B *and* D *go to laptop.*

B   Significantly.

A   *How* significantly?

D   Across the board.

        Beat.

B   So…?

A   What do we…?

Beat.

E   We leave it.

D   What about the community reps?

E   Ignore them. Let it blow over.

D   Okay.

B   Cool.

A   Great.

They gather their things in silence. They start leaving the room.

C   (*Handing notes to* A.) Your notes.

They all exit.

WORD ASSOCIATION

Characters: A, B, C, D, E.

A   Table.

B   Wood.

A   Trees.

B   Leaves.

A   Autumn.

B   Winter.

A   Summer.

B   Sunshine.

A   Island.

B   Ocean.

A   Waves.

B   Surfing.

A   Internet.

B   Emails.

A   Work.

B   Mondays.

A   Weekends.

B   Dancing.

A   Feet.

B   Shoes.

A   Heels.

B   Fashion.

A   Models.

B   Bodies.

C   *Dead*.

     Beat.

A   Accident.

B   Car.

A   Crash.

B   Course.

A   Learning.

B   School.

A   Friends.

B   Gossip.

A   Columns.

B   Magazines.

A   Pictures.

B   Articles.

A   News.

D   *Fake*.

    Beat.

B   Real.

A   Unreal.

B   Story.

A   Plot.

B   Twist.

A   Turn.

B   Wheel.

A   Round.

B   Globe.

A   World.

B   Countries.

A   Cities.

B   People.

A   Crowds.

B   Communities.

E   *Influx*.

         Beat.

C   Mass.

D   Overflow.

A   Cup.

C   Half.

B   Empty.

D   Cup.

A   Half.

E   *Full*.

         Beat.

C   Circle.

D   Spin.

E   Turn.

C   Take.

D   Give.

E   Back.

D   Revoke.

         Beat.

         Territories
         Occupied
         Disputed
         Apartheid
         Security
         Neighbourhood
         Settlement

Attack
Retaliation
Occupation
Pre-emptive
Prevention
Prevent
Clash
War
Rebels
Identity
Crisis
Genocide
Premeditated
Identity
Identify
Crisis
Prove
Woke
Up
Crisis
Wokeness
Can't
Say
Strike
Rights
Disruption
Workers
Capital
Religion
British
Values
Preventable
Evils
Country
Changed
Whip
On
Settlement
Rivers
Blood

Key
Workers
Clap
Mind
Gap
Pay
Gap
Play
Party
Through
Gate
Deaths
Sorry
Not-Sorry
Thems
The
Violent
Violence
State
Defence
Still
Here
Armed
Bride
Choice
Witch
Say
Sorry
Feel
Sorry
Be
Sorry
Values
Threat
Nation
State
No
Home
Now
Home

Less
Try
Harder
Scrounger
Benefits
Scam
Generations
Help
Arrivals
Build
Ships
Passengers
Rush
Visitors
Now
You're
Done
Exit
Leave
Stay
Stayed
Delayed
Homes
Houses
Child
Pupil
Integrate
Escape
Failed
Thousands
Thousands
Thousands
Millions
Into
Stay
Stop
Sham
Suspect
Suspected
Borders

Flood
Influx
Unskilled
Drain
Stain
Flood
Failed
Temporary
Re-educate
Re-education
Better
Now
Speak
Normal
Population
School
Done
Leader
Done
Breaking
Done
Point
Done
Boats
Done
Influx
Done
Waves
Done

NORMAL 3 – NIGHT

Characters: A, B, C, D, E.

WhatsApp scene.

This scene can be played as simply words being said in a group.

A   Literature…

B   Music…

C   Instruments…

D   Art…

E   History…

A   Discoveries…

B   Mathematics…

C   Geometry…

D   Patterns…

E   Calligraphy…

A   Architecture…

B   Shapes…

C   Monuments…

D   Museums…

E   Mosques…

A   Minarets…

B   Ceramics…

C   Sculptures…

D   Prayers…

E   Verses…

A   Cosmos…

B   Poetry…

C   Films…

D   Clothes…

E   Fabrics…

A   Colours…

B   Jewellery…

C   Charity…

D   Festivals…

E   Global cultures…

A   Mashallah for compliments…

B   Inshallah for hope. And literally everything else.

C   Bismillah for beginnings…

D   The echo of the azaan.

E   Fasting…

A   Pilgrimage…

B   Wishing peace on people when you meet them…

C   Wishing peace on them when we leave them.

E   Praying.

A   Our foods…

B   And that we eat them *every* day.

C   Yeah! Not just on a Friday.

D   Our festivals…

B   Our festival *foods*.

E   Eid…

B   Eid *food*!

E   I swear that's all you talk about.

A   I *love* how much we love feeding people.

D   Yeah. When someone comes over, they can't leave without eating *something*.

A   I love our teas…

B   And our snacks.

A   But *sometimes* tea and cake. #BritishStyle.

D   I love the games we used to play as kids.

A   Different fashion…

C   *Hijabi* fashion.

B   Hijabi make-up…

A   Halal restaurants…

B   *Mango* season!

A   How we celebrate *moments*.

D   Our normal. As in, all of that. Everything we've all said.
      Every single thing. Our *normal*. I love that the *most*.

STONES

Characters: A (*female*).

A   My daughter, Iman, loves to build things. She used to do it *all* the time.

She would run around the house finding various bits and pieces. She'd gather them one at a time in her tiny little hands, and lay them out until she'd made a particular pattern. And then she'd tell me with *such* confidence –

'Mummy, this is our house'…
or,
'Mummy, this is my school'…
'Mummy, this is the <u>world</u>.'

And I'd say, *'Yes, my sweet. It is.'*

Beat.

To be honest with you, all I could see is a stack of discarded things she'd piled up, one on top of the other. Just *things*.

I didn't see our house, like *she* did. But I'd be *fascinated* by *her* fascination. She's a *wonder* to me.

Beat.

I took Iman to see my parents last year. To meet her *grandparents* for the first time. She'd never left the country before.

When we got there, my parents were waiting outside the door for us. And oh, they *loved* her. They *loved* her as *soon* as they saw her. And she loved them *right* back. *Straight* away. Even without really *knowing* them yet.

In the entire time we were there, if I raised my voice even a *little* towards her, my parents told me off. Like *I* was a child again. They said,

'Whilst she's here, she is ours. And we don't give you permission to raise your voice at her.'

It's the first time I realised how *special* the love is
between grandparent and grandchild. It's love in its
purest form.

Beat.

For the two weeks we were there, she managed to get
them involved in her love of building things. But this
time, instead of *objects*, she wanted to use *stones*. So,
every morning, all three of them would head outside to
collect *stones* of *different* sizes, shapes and colours. And
after a while, I'd see them walking back from the
window. Their hands cupped against their chests. Hands
full of *stones*.

Then the three of us would watch Iman as she sat on the
floor building 'two houses' with the stones. One that was
our house,

'*Where we live.*'

And one which was *this* house,

'*Where Nana and Nano live.*'

And even though I still *only* saw a pile of stones, my
parents *swore* they saw *exactly* what she did.

Beat.

They were *devastated* when we were leaving. And *Iman*
was devastated. I felt *cruel* separating them from each
other. But we all have to go back home some time…
Right?

Beat.

Iman wanted to take all the stones back with her. I told
her we couldn't. So, my parents found a solution.

They picked out two stones. The '*best ones*' they said.
And using chalk, they wrote Iman's name on one stone,
and their names on the other. They wrote them in our
mother tongue.

Iman was *mesmerised*. Her name in a *different* language.
Her name even *more* beautiful. Like she became a

bigger person. There were now *multiple* versions of her. And she *loved* them *all*.

Beat.

On her first day back to school, she refused to let go of the stones. I was worried she would drop them. So I said,

'*Let's put our hands together, and we will hold them in the middle of our palms.*'

The entire walk to school, the stones made little knocking sounds. It felt like her nana and nano were trying to tell us something.

Beat.

At the end of the day, when it was time to collect her again, I waited at the school gates. All the parents had seen and taken their children home. But I couldn't see Iman anywhere.

That's when her teacher approached me. Told me that Iman is inside. She must have seen fear suddenly fill my face. Because she quickly said, '*Iman is fine,*' but that I would have to come inside before I could see her.

Beat.

She didn't say a word until we arrived in a small, cramped office. That's when she told me that two police officers and a social worker were with Iman. *Questioning* her. When I asked why, she refused to tell me. Simply that they will speak to me after they had spoken to Iman.

I waited. Pacing the room the entire time. *Terrified*. And when the two officers finally opened the door, Iman wasn't with them.

'*Please sit down. You can see Iman in a moment.*'

I did as they asked.

Is Iman okay?

'*There have been some concerns about Iman's recent trip abroad.*'

I asked them to elaborate.

'*Why did you travel there?*'

To see my parents...

'*Are you a British citizen?*'

Yes. I have a British passport... Who is with Iman?

'*What about Iman?*'

She was born here... She's not alone, is she? She doesn't like being alone.

'*Why did you name her that? Iman.*'

My husband has always loved that name.

'*What does it mean?*'

Faith. It means faith...

'*...We know.*'

Iman usually eats at this time. She must be hungry.

'*Iman's grandparents. What were they teaching her out there?*'

What do you mean?

They put a piece of paper in front of me. I recognised straight away that it was Iman's work.

'*What is this?*'

It's a drawing. Of Iman with her grandparents.

'*What are they holding?*'

Stones.

'*Hmm.*'

They stayed silent for a few moments.

What exactly is the problem?

They turned the page over. And pointed to some words that Iman had written. My heart soared. Because I could see she had tried to write her name, '*Iman*', like her grandparents had written it. In our *mother tongue*.

'*What does this say?*'

'*Iman.' It's her name. In our mother tongue.*

'*She speaks her mother tongue?*'

Not really.

'*Why did she write it then?*'

Because she knows the spelling of her name now. In her mother tongue.

'*Right…*'

It was then they placed Iman's stones on the table in front of me.

'*What are these?*'

Stones. Like the ones she drew on the paper.

'*Iman said her grandparents gave them to her?*'

Yes. She likes to build things with them.

'*Things like what?*'

She pretends they are houses.

'*That doesn't make a lot of sense.*'

She has an imagination.

'*Iman has returned from another country. And she has carried these with her into school. Can you see what the problem with that could be?*'

No. I don't. They're stones. Just stones.

'*Iman wouldn't give them to her teacher. She said they were from her grandparents. They have this writing on them. The same as on the paper. Can you see why her teacher might have felt… concerned?*'

By a child? No. I can't.

'*You can't see what the problem is?*'

Please explain. Because I don't see it.

'We're simply trying to <u>prevent</u> anyone going down any... Well, you know the stories. British citizens. Schoolgirls. An interest in other languages can be... concerning.'

Can I see Iman now?

'Does your husband interact with any faith institutions?'

Yes. For prayer...

'There can be a lot of bad people in these places.'

I don't... Please, can I see my daughter now?

'What are your thoughts on some of the acts committed by members of your community?'

I told them. *I condemned.*

'Do you know that these things happen because of certain verses of your holy book?'

I don't think... I wasn't sure if I was supposed to apologise...

I noticed then that one of them had started moving Iman's stones around on the table. Playing with them. *Carelessly.* Like they were *nothing.*

Can you give those stones back please? They are Iman's.

'You're being a little uncooperative now. Is everything okay?'

Everything is okay. I want to see my daughter. That's all.

'Of course. We're not trying to keep you from Iman. But we do need to ask some more questions before you can see her.'

What questions?

'They will be familiar to you. Since you are now a citizen.'

Before I could ask anything else, words were fired at me...

'Which two houses fought in the Wars of the Roses?'

I don't…

'What did Sir Frank Whittle invent in the 1930s?'

I'm not… sure.

'Who was given the title of Lord Protector?'

I can't…

'Under which king did the Anglo-Saxon kingdoms in England unite to defeat the Vikings?'

'Who was supported by clansmen from the Scottish Highlands and raised an army in 1745?'

'In which country of the British Empire did the Boer War, 1899 to 1902 take place?'

'Where are the Crown Jewels kept?'

'Where does the Fringe festival take place?'

'What stories are associated with Geoffrey Chaucer?'

'What did the Habeas Corpus Act introduce?'

'When is St David's Day?'

'How many members does the Welsh Government have?'

'What percentage of the UK population has a parent or grandparent born outside of the UK?'

Please stop! I want to see my daughter. My daughter. Right now. I want to see my daughter right now! Stop! Please stop! Please, please, please stop… Just stop! STOP!

Beat.

It took them another twenty minutes to return after they left me in the room alone again. They left Iman's stones on the table. I held them close to my chest and waited. And when they came back, they brought Iman with them. Her eyes wide. Fear *cracked* into them. My daughter. Already *cracked*.

'We've made our assessment. We have no more concerns. You and Iman can go. But we advise you to think carefully about how the things you do can be seen by others. Be more considerate next time. And don't let Iman get too caught up in her mother tongue. It can lead to "other" paths.'

They walked away. And I held Iman close. I held her closer than I've ever held her.

I hadn't realised I'd been gripping Iman's stones tightly in my hands the whole time. They left an imprint. On my palm.

Beat.

Iman can't bear to look at stones any more. She builds no more houses. She builds nothing any more.

Beat.

My parents still go out to collect stones for Iman, for when she returns. They say there's a pile as tall as her in a corner of their house.

(*She opens her palm to reveal a stone.*) I see it now. In the stone. The world. Iman's world.

Do you see it?

When she's ready, I'll give the world to her.

To Iman. *My* Iman.

End of play.

A Nick Hern Book

Word-Play first published in Great Britain in 2023 as a paperback original by Nick Hern Books Limited, The Glasshouse, 49a Goldhawk Road, London W12 8QP, in association with the Royal Court Theatre, London

Cover artwork by Louise Richardson

Designed and typeset by Nick Hern Books, London
Printed in Great Britain by Mimeo Ltd, Huntingdon, Cambridgeshire PE29 6XX

A CIP catalogue record for this book is available from the British Library

ISBN 978 1 83904 131 0

www.nickhernbooks.co.uk/environmental-policy

www.nickhernbooks.co.uk

facebook.com/nickhernbooks

twitter.com/nickhernbooks